EASY POP MELODIES

FOR TROMBONE

ISBN 978-1-4803-8433-0

HAL•LEONARD®
CORPORATION

7777 W. BLUEMOUND RD. P.O. BOX 13819 MILWAUKEE, WI 53213

Visit Hal Leonard Online at
www.halleonard.com

4	All My Loving
5	Beauty and the Beast
6	Blowin' in the Wind
7	Can You Feel the Love Tonight
8	Can't Help Falling in Love
9	Clocks
10	Daydream Believer
11	Don't Know Why
12	Don't Stop Believin'
14	Edelweiss
15	Eight Days a Week
16	Every Breath You Take
17	Fireflies
18	Georgia on My Mind
20	Hey, Soul Sister
22	Hot N Cold
19	In My Life
24	Isn't She Lovely
25	The Letter
26	Like a Virgin
27	The Look of Love
28	Love Me Tender
30	Love Story
29	Mr. Tambourine Man
32	Moon River
33	Morning Has Broken
34	My Cherie Amour
36	My Favorite Things
35	My Girl
38	My Heart Will Go On (Love Theme from 'Titanic')
39	Nights in White Satin
40	Nowhere Man
41	Puff the Magic Dragon
42	Raindrops Keep Fallin' on My Head
43	Scarborough Fair/Canticle
44	Somewhere Out There
46	The Sound of Music
48	Strangers in the Night
49	Sunshine on My Shoulders
50	Sweet Caroline
51	Till There Was You
52	The Times They Are A-Changin'
54	Tomorrow
53	Unchained Melody
56	Viva la Vida
58	We Are the World
59	What a Wonderful World
60	Wonderwall
62	You Are the Sunshine of My Life
63	You've Got a Friend

ALL MY LOVING

TROMBONE

Words and Music by JOHN LENNON
and PAUL McCARTNEY

BEAUTY AND THE BEAST

from Walt Disney's BEAUTY AND THE BEAST

TROMBONE

Lyrics by HOWARD ASHMAN
Music by ALAN MENKEN

BLOWIN' IN THE WIND

TROMBONE

Words and Music by
BOB DYLAN

CAN YOU FEEL THE LOVE TONIGHT
from Walt Disney Pictures' THE LION KING

TROMBONE

Music by ELTON JOHN
Lyrics by TIM RICE

CAN'T HELP FALLING IN LOVE

TROMBONE

Words and Music by GEORGE DAVID WEISS,
HUGO PERETTI and LUIGI CREATORE

CLOCKS

Words and Music by GUY BERRYMAN,
JON BUCKLAND, WILL CHAMPION
and CHRIS MARTIN

TROMBONE

DAYDREAM BELIEVER

TROMBONE

Words and Music by
JOHN STEWART

DON'T KNOW WHY

TROMBONE

Words and Music by
JESSE HARRIS

DON'T STOP BELIEVIN'

TROMBONE

Words and Music by STEVE PERRY,
NEAL SCHON and JONATHAN CAIN

EDELWEISS
from THE SOUND OF MUSIC

TROMBONE

Lyrics by OSCAR HAMMERSTEIN II
Music by RICHARD RODGERS

EIGHT DAYS A WEEK

TROMBONE

Words and Music by JOHN LENNON
and PAUL McCARTNEY

EVERY BREATH YOU TAKE

TROMBONE

Music and Lyrics by
STING

FIREFLIES

TROMBONE

Words and Music by
ADAM YOUNG

GEORGIA ON MY MIND

TROMBONE

Words by STUART GORRELL
Music by HOAGY CARMICHAEL

IN MY LIFE

TROMBONE

Words and Music by JOHN LENNON
and PAUL McCARTNEY

HEY, SOUL SISTER

TROMBONE

Words and Music by PAT MONAHAN,
ESPEN LIND and AMUND BJORKLAND

I knew when we col - lid - ed you're the one I have de - cid - ed who's one of my kind. __
I be - lieve in you; like a vir - gin, you're Ma - don - na, and I'm al - ways gon - na

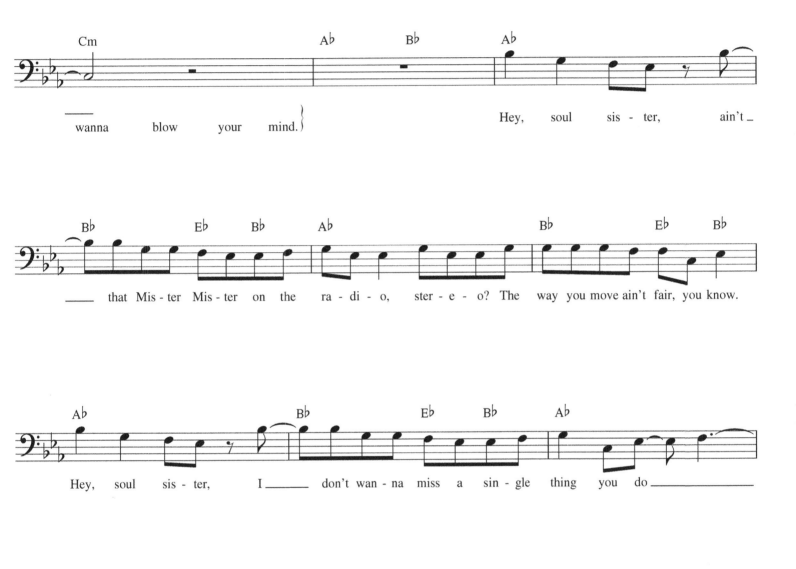

wanna blow your mind.
Hey, soul sis - ter, ain't __

__ that Mis - ter Mis - ter on the ra - di - o, ster - e - o? The way you move ain't fair, you know.

Hey, soul sis - ter, I _____ don't wan - na miss a sin - gle thing you do _____

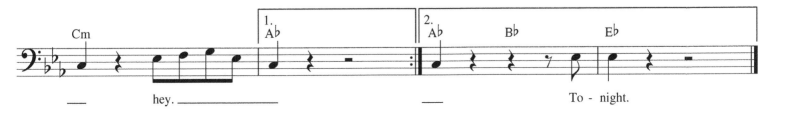

__ to - night. Hey, _____ hey, _____

__ hey. _____ To - night.

HOT N COLD

TROMBONE

Words and Music by KATY PERRY,
MAX MARTIN and LUKASZ GOTTWALD

ISN'T SHE LOVELY

TROMBONE

Words and Music by
STEVIE WONDER

THE LETTER

TROMBONE

Words and Music by
WAYNE CARSON THOMPSON

LIKE A VIRGIN

TROMBONE

Words and Music by BILLY STEINBERG
and TOM KELLY

THE LOOK OF LOVE
from CASINO ROYALE

TROMBONE

Words by HAL DAVID
Music by BURT BACHARACH

LOVE ME TENDER

TROMBONE

Words and Music by ELVIS PRESLEY
and VERA MATSON

MR. TAMBOURINE MAN

TROMBONE

Words and Music by
BOB DYLAN

LOVE STORY

TROMBONE

Words and Music by
TAYLOR SWIFT

MOON RIVER

from the Paramount Picture BREAKFAST AT TIFFANY'S

TROMBONE

Words by JOHNNY MERCER
Music by HENRY MANCINI

MORNING HAS BROKEN

TROMBONE

Words by ELEANOR FARJEON
Music by CAT STEVENS

MY CHERIE AMOUR

TROMBONE

Words and Music by STEVIE WONDER,
SYLVIA MOY and HENRY COSBY

MY GIRL

TROMBONE

Words and Music by WILLIAM "SMOKEY" ROBINSON
and RONALD WHITE

MY FAVORITE THINGS

from THE SOUND OF MUSIC

TROMBONE

Lyrics by OSCAR HAMMERSTEIN II
Music by RICHARD RODGERS

MY HEART WILL GO ON
(Love Theme from 'Titanic')
from the Paramount and Twentieth Century Fox Motion Picture TITANIC

Music by JAMES HORNER
Lyric by WILL JENNINGS

TROMBONE

NIGHTS IN WHITE SATIN

TROMBONE

Words and Music by
JUSTIN HAYWARD

NOWHERE MAN

TROMBONE

Words and Music by JOHN LENNON
and PAUL McCARTNEY

PUFF THE MAGIC DRAGON

TROMBONE

Words and Music by LENNY LIPTON
and PETER YARROW

RAINDROPS KEEP FALLIN' ON MY HEAD
from BUTCH CASSIDY AND THE SUNDANCE KID

TROMBONE

Lyric by HAL DAVID
Music by BURT BACHARACH

SCARBOROUGH FAIR/CANTICLE

TROMBONE

Arrangement and Original Counter Melody by PAUL SIMON
and ARTHUR GARFUNKEL

Somewhere Out There

from AN AMERICAN TAIL

TROMBONE

Music by BARRY MANN and JAMES HORNER
Lyric by CYNTHIA WEIL

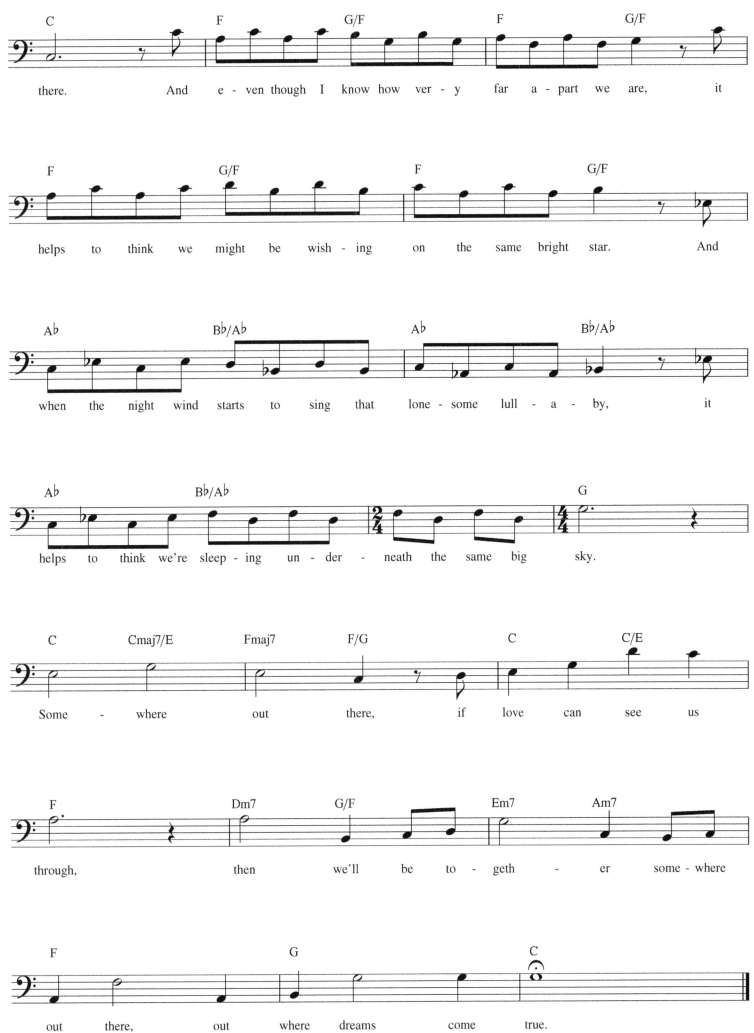

THE SOUND OF MUSIC

from THE SOUND OF MUSIC

TROMBONE

Lyrics by OSCAR HAMMERSTEIN II
Music by RICHARD RODGERS

STRANGERS IN THE NIGHT
adapted from A MAN COULD GET KILLED

TROMBONE

Words by CHARLES SINGLETON and EDDIE SNYDER
Music by BERT KAEMPFERT

SUNSHINE ON MY SHOULDERS

TROMBONE

Words by JOHN DENVER
Music by JOHN DENVER, MIKE TAYLOR
and DICK KNISS

SWEET CAROLINE

TROMBONE

Words and Music by
NEIL DIAMOND

TILL THERE WAS YOU
from Meredith Willson's THE MUSIC MAN

TROMBONE

By MEREDITH WILLSON

THE TIMES THEY ARE A-CHANGIN'

TROMBONE

Words and Music by
BOB DYLAN

UNCHAINED MELODY

Lyric by HY ZARET
Music by ALEX NORTH

TROMBONE

TOMORROW
from The Musical Production ANNIE

TROMBONE

Lyric by MARTIN CHARNIN
Music by CHARLES STROUSE

VIVA LA VIDA

TROMBONE

Words and Music by GUY BERRYMAN,
JON BUCKLAND, WILL CHAMPION
and CHRIS MARTIN

WE ARE THE WORLD

TROMBONE

Words and Music by LIONEL RICHIE
and MICHAEL JACKSON

WHAT A WONDERFUL WORLD

TROMBONE

Words and Music by GEORGE DAVID WEISS
and BOB THIELE

WONDERWALL

TROMBONE

Words and Music by
NOEL GALLAGHER

YOU ARE THE SUNSHINE OF MY LIFE

TROMBONE

Words and Music by
STEVIE WONDER

YOU'VE GOT A FRIEND

TROMBONE

Words and Music by
CAROLE KING

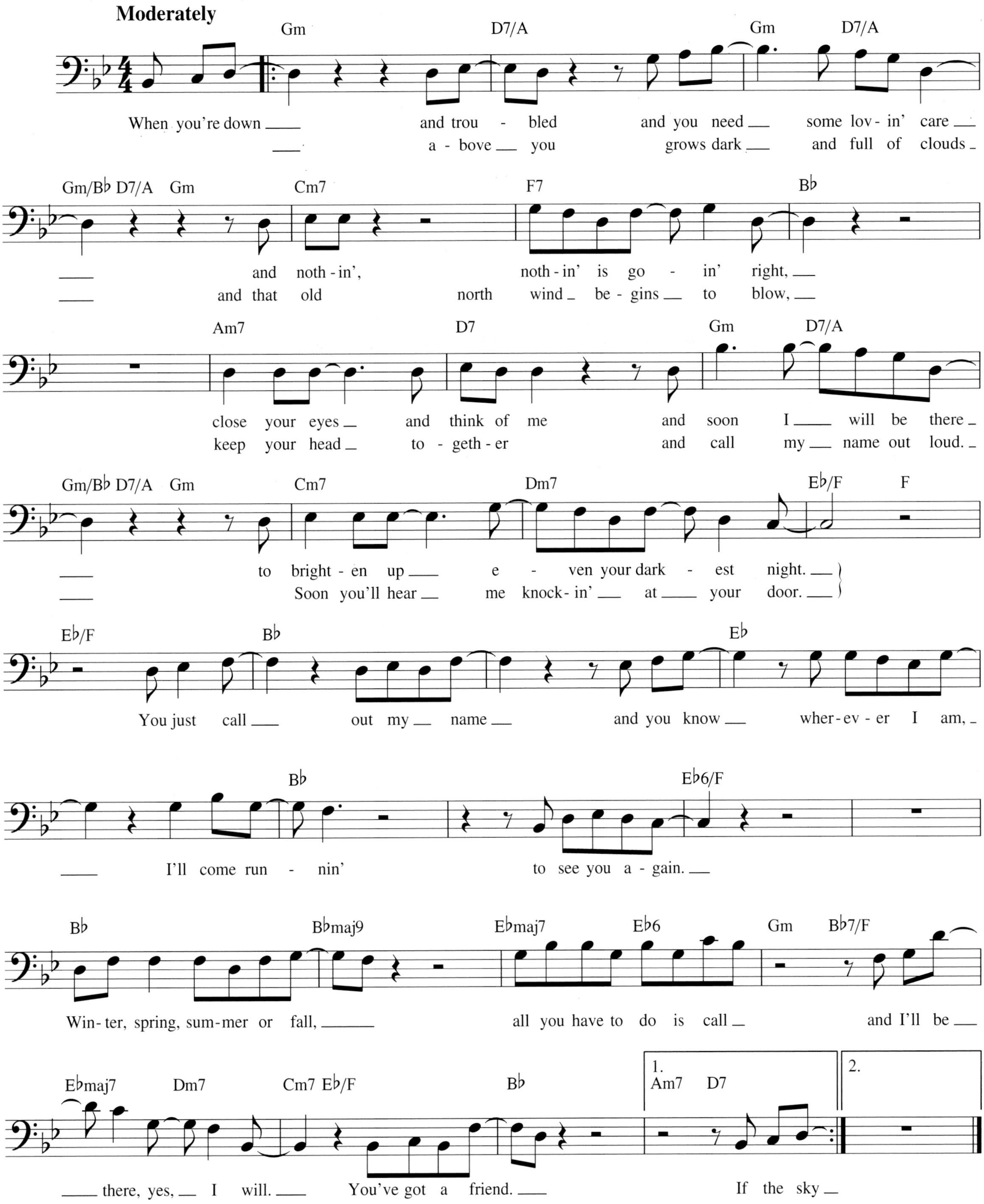

HAL·LEONARD
EASY INSTRUMENTAL PLAY-ALONG

- Perfect for beginning players
- Carefully edited to include only the notes and rhythms that students learn in the first months playing their instrument

- Great-sounding demonstration and play-along tracks
- Audio tracks can be accessed online for download or streaming, using the unique code inside the book

DISNEY

Book with Online Audio Tracks

The Ballad of Davy Crockett • Can You Feel the Love Tonight • Candle on the Water • I Just Can't Wait to Be King • The Medallion Calls • Mickey Mouse March • Part of Your World • Whistle While You Work • You Can Fly! You Can Fly! You Can Fly! • You'll Be in My Heart (Pop Version).

00122184	Flute	$9.99
00122185	Clarinet	$9.99
00122186	Alto Sax	$9.99
00122187	Tenor Sax	$9.99
00122188	Trumpet	$9.99
00122189	Horn	$9.99
00122190	Trombone	$9.99
00122191	Violin	$9.99
00122192	Viola	$9.99
00122193	Cello	$9.99
00122194	Keyboard Percussion	$9.99

CLASSIC ROCK

Book with Online Audio Tracks

Another One Bites the Dust • Born to Be Wild • Brown Eyed Girl • Dust in the Wind • Every Breath You Take • Fly like an Eagle • I Heard It Through the Grapevine • I Shot the Sheriff • Oye Como Va • Up Around the Bend.

00122195	Flute	$9.99
00122196	Clarinet	$9.99
00122197	Alto Sax	$9.99
00122198	Tenor Sax	$9.99
00122201	Trumpet	$9.99
00122202	Horn	$9.99
00122203	Trombone	$9.99
00122205	Violin	$9.99
00122206	Viola	$9.99
00122207	Cello	$9.99
00122208	Keyboard Percussion	$9.99

CLASSICAL THEMES

Book with Online Audio Tracks

Can Can • Carnival of Venice • Finlandia • Largo from Symphony No. 9 ("New World") • Morning • Musette in D Major • Ode to Joy • Spring • Symphony No. 1 in C Minor, Fourth Movement Excerpt • Trumpet Voluntary.

00123108	Flute	$9.99
00123109	Clarinet	$9.99
00123110	Alto Sax	$9.99
00123111	Tenor Sax	$9.99
00123112	Trumpet	$9.99
00123113	Horn	$9.99
00123114	Trombone	$9.99
00123115	Violin	$9.99
00123116	Viola	$9.99
00123117	Cello	$9.99
00123118	Keyboard Percussion	$9.99

CHRISTMAS CAROLS

Book with Online Audio Tracks

Angels We Have Heard on High • Christ Was Born on Christmas Day • Come, All Ye Shepherds • Come, Thou Long-Expected Jesus • Good Christian Men, Rejoice • Jingle Bells • Jolly Old St. Nicholas • Lo, How a Rose E'er Blooming • On Christmas Night • Up on the Housetop.

00130363	Flute	$9.99
00130364	Clarinet	$9.99
00130365	Alto Sax	$9.99
00130366	Tenor Sax	$9.99
00130367	Trumpet	$9.99
00130368	Horn	$9.99
00130369	Trombone	$9.99
00130370	Violin	$9.99
00130371	Viola	$9.99
00130372	Cello	$9.99
00130373	Keyboard Percussion	$9.99

POP FAVORITES

Book with Online Audio Tracks

Achy Breaky Heart (Don't Tell My Heart) • I'm a Believer • Imagine • Jailhouse Rock • La Bamba • Louie, Louie • Ob-La-Di, Ob-La-Da • Splish Splash • Stand by Me • Yellow Submarine.

00232231	Flute	$9.99
00232232	Clarinet	$9.99
00232233	Alto Sax	$9.99
00232234	Tenor Sax	$9.99
00232235	Trumpet	$9.99
00232236	Horn	$9.99
00232237	Trombone	$9.99
00232238	Violin	$9.99
00232239	Viola	$9.99
00232240	Cello	$9.99
00233296	Keyboard Percussion	$9.99

Disney characters and artwork © Disney Enterprises, Inc.

www.halleonard.com

Prices, content, and availability subject to change without notice.